September 2005

W9-CPE-178

Ed & Anita,

Thank you for the many contributions you made to our building and, more importantly, our life together at King of Kings. We hope that you don't remember us only as the "project you left early" but as the people who valued your presence and held you and your family in prayer.

We hope this book adds to the fond memories you take with you from here. Be assured that you will long be remembered for your love & faithful Spirit.

Pastor & People of
King of Kings

# HUDSON RIVER
# JOURNEY

# HUDSON RIVER JOURNEY

## Images from Lake Tear of the Clouds to New York Harbor

PHOTOGRAPHS BY HARDIE TRUESDALE

TEXT BY JOANNE MICHAELS

Foreword by Pete Seeger

Introduction by Riverkeeper Alex Matthiessen

THE COUNTRYMAN PRESS

WOODSTOCK, VERMONT

DEDICATION

To the memory of C. W. Truesdale
—H. T.

For my son, Erik, who intends to enter the political arena and make changes
in a system he has often heard me lament during his two decades on Earth.
—J. M.

———————

Library of Congress Cataloging-in-Publication Data:
Truesdale, Hardie.
Hudson River journey : images from Lake Tear of the Clouds to New York Harbor / images by Hardie Truesdale ; text by Joanne Michaels ;
foreword by Pete Seeger ; introduction by Alex Matthiessen.
p. cm.  ISBN 0-88150-594-3
1. Hudson River (N.Y. and N.J.)—Pictorial works. 2. Hudson River Valley (N.Y. and N.J.)—Pictorial works. 3. Hudson River (N.Y., and N.J.)—Description and travel.
4. Hudson River Valley (N.Y. and N.J.)—Description and travel. 5. Hudson River Valley (N.Y. and N.J.)—History, Local—Pictorial works. 6. Natural history—
Hudson River Valley (N.Y. and N.J.)—Pictorial works. I. Michaels, Joanne, 1950– II. Title.
F127.H8T88 2003
917.47'30444—dc21    2003048590

Book design by Susan McClellan
Published by The Countryman Press, P.O. Box 748, Woodstock, Vermont 05091
Distributed by W.W. Norton & Company, Inc., 500 Fifth Avenue, New York, NY 10110
Printed in Spain by Artes Graficas Toledo
10 9 8 7 6 5 4 3

# CONTENTS

*Foreword* by Pete Seeger  7

*Introduction* by Riverkeeper Alex Matthiessen  8

*Going with the Flow* by Joanne Michaels  9

Acknowledgments  11

Hudson River Journey  12

*Directions:* If You Want to Go  118

▲ SLOOP CLEARWATER

The sloop *Clearwater* sailing
the Hudson River

# FOREWORD

HUDSON RIVER JOURNEY will help you to know your river valley better. Don't just read it; pick out a day (and a raindate) when you can put on hiking shoes and visit some of these places yourself! We are all lucky to live in one of the most remarkable regions of the world.

Take it easy, but take it, as my old time friend Woody Guthrie said. . . . He's the man who wrote the song:

*This land is your land;*

*This land is my land.*

—Pete Seeger
Beacon, New York

# INTRODUCTION

**H**UDSON RIVER JOURNEY is a celebration of America's first river and the people and history that continue to make the Hudson one of the country's premiere heritage sites. From a tranquil clear-water pond in the Adirondacks to the roiling waters off the Battery at the southern tip of Manhattan, the Hudson courses its way through some of the most magnificent scenery and important historic places in America.

Joanne Michaels, prolific author and dedicated purveyor of useful guides, has brought us a book that will both delight and inform. A passionate and fierce advocate of the Hudson River Valley, Michaels and photographer Hardie Truesdale have brought together words and images to highlight some of the many places that make the Hudson majestic and draw visitors from around the globe. With a masterful use of light that sometimes bathes, at other times dances with, his subject, Truesdale captures the sublime beauty of the Hudson Valley and its most compelling vistas and landmarks.

This book comes at a crucial juncture in the ongoing struggle to reclaim the Hudson from its would-be despoilers. The very environmental laws that thirty years ago gave citizens the right and ability to stop polluters are now under assault by the federal government. If something is not done to stem the anti-environmental tide that is gripping Washington, all the gains of the past thirty years will be lost and the nearly restored Hudson will become imperiled once again. It is critical that we enlist the support of the people and visitors of the Hudson Valley to roll up their sleeves and help do the work necessary to safeguard the laws that protect the Hudson River and that protect us.

This book will not only re-inspire the loyalty of longtime Hudson Valley advocates, but will spawn a whole new constituency of river defenders. They too will come to understand that the way forward is not to repeat the mistakes of the past but to preserve that which makes the Hudson Valley unique and economically sustainable: its rich history and natural splendor. For their role in helping enlist new recruits to the Hudson River cause, Michaels and Truesdale will take their place among the heroes of the Hudson.

Riverkeeper Alex Matthiessen
Garrison, New York

# GOING WITH THE FLOW

G O OUT ON THE HUDSON RIVER and discover why Native Americans called it "the river that flows both ways." One hot, humid summer afternoon, friends in Dutchess County invited me along on the maiden voyage of their rebuilt sailboat. For a couple of hours we enjoyed gliding north, cool drinks in hand, heading toward Kingston's Rondout waterfront district, where we planned to stop for lunch. But the stitching on the mainsail seam gave way, and we decided it was best to motor back to the marina. As the key was being turned to start the engine, it snapped off in the ignition. Suddenly, our relaxed Sunday outing was transformed into an unexpected adventure.

It was then that I first experienced the Hudson in all its glory. One minute the boat was gently rocking shoreward. Moments later, amazingly strong winds sent us flying in the opposite direction. I began to feel queasy, compelled to lie down to ease the effect of the river's relentless, unpredictable motion. Luckily, within an hour (a seemingly endless period of time, especially when one is in a horizontal position, below the deck), a fellow boater who had received our SOS via radio towed us safely to shore.

I look at the Hudson differently now, whether I am crossing the river via the Kingston–Rhinecliff Bridge, or atop one of the Catskill peaks gazing down at magnificent vistas. I learned in grade school that the Hudson River is a tidal estuary, but I never understood what the description really meant. That day on the sailboat, I felt the changing tides. And tides are a rarity in a river.

The Hudson is an anomaly in yet another way: it contains both fresh and salt water, continually churning together. Even on fairly calm summer days, winds can arise quickly, seemingly out of nowhere, creating a dynamic, ever-changing waterway. From its origins at Lake Tear of the Clouds (altitude 4,293 feet) in the Adirondacks, to sea level in Manhattan, 315 miles to the south, the river is full of surprises. I wondered what Henry Hudson and his crew thought and felt as they sailed northward in September 1609.

Those of us who reside in the valleys and mountains and usually view the Hudson from afar should consider getting down to the riverside. Head out in a kayak or on a sailboat one day. Or simply sit and carefully observe from the shoreline. Experience the contradictions and raw beauty of this treasure in our midst.

"I think it an invaluable advantage to be born and brought up in the neighborhood of some grand and noble object in nature: a river, a lake or a mountain," remarked Washington Irving more than a century ago. "We make a friendship with it; we, in a manner, ally ourselves with it for life." I couldn't agree more.

Come, take a Hudson River journey . . .

Joanne Michaels

### ▲ FALL MIST, SKYTOP

When we see photographs of rivers, mountains, breathtaking scenery, they are frozen in time, seemingly static. But the natural world of the Hudson Valley and Catskills is as much about dynamic change as it is about tranquil beauty. For a collection of images, I wanted the spirit of both aspects of the area captured. So I turned to Hardie Truesdale, a photographer renowned for his phenomenal Shawangunk landscapes—and extraordinary eye. Hardie will wait for hours until a particular view is bathed in just the right light, before pointing the camera. His vision conveys the magic of the region through an ineffable mixture of nature, timing, and judgment. Truesdale, an outdoorsman and Hudson Valley resident for twenty-five years, speaks volumes with his magnificent photographs.

# ACKNOWLEDGMENTS

MY HEARTFELT GRATITUDE to all the people of the Hudson Valley and Catskills who have spoken up and fought difficult battles to save what we have here against formidable corporate opponents, including Con Edison, General Electric, and St. Lawrence Cement, as well as some real estate developers and the government of the United States. Many of you did this in a time when such concerns were unpopular. I want to thank those citizens, organizations, and political representatives who continue the fight to preserve the heritage and beauty of this special place on the planet. Without all of you, the phenomenal images in this book would not exist.

Pete Seeger, now 84, has been a torchbearer in this struggle for nearly forty years. He has inspired generations through his music, and by his courage to face the opposition head-on with the facts—sprinkled with a heavy dose of humor and common sense! The Hudson River sloop *Clearwater*, started by Seeger and other Hudson Valley citizens in 1966, has as its mission to restore the river. When I see the *Clearwater* these days sailing on the Hudson, it is a reminder of all we have achieved in cleaning up the river, and all we have yet to accomplish. I am grateful to people like Pete and Riverkeeper Alex Matthiessen for what they have done for everyone, enriching our appreciation of the Hudson. I also salute them for getting us down to the waterfront for festivals and seasonal celebrations, so that we experience firsthand the power and beauty of the Hudson River.

All Americans must remain vigilant, and pay close attention to environmental issues, particularly at this time when rivers, mountains, forests, and oceans are being threatened unlike ever before, particularly by threats from within our nation. I urge all of you to become involved in the ongoing preservation efforts, so that the photographs in this book do not end up as history, but continue to reflect the magnificent scenery and unique character of the Hudson Valley and Catskill Mountains.

Joanne Michaels

## ▲ WINDSURFING ON THE HUDSON

## ▶ ADIRONDACK VIEWS FROM MOUNT MARCY

The Van Hoevenberg Trail in the Adirondack Preserve leads to a small lake about halfway up the southwestern slope of Mount Marcy, the highest peak in New York State. The Native Americans named this body of water, 4,293 feet above sea level, Lake Tear of the Clouds. Although the Hudson River originates from several springs in the Adirondacks that supply three of its branches, Lake Tear of the Clouds is acknowledged to be the Hudson's main source and point of origin. The only way to reach the lake is to hike in.

### ◀ INDIAN LAKE SUNRISE

One of several lakes in the Adirondack Preserve, Indian Lake reflects the tranquil origins of the Hudson River. This photograph was taken from the western shore of the lake looking east.

### ▶ BLUE LEDGE TRAIL

This autumn scene in the Adirondack Preserve evokes the humble beginnings of the Hudson, a stark contrast to the river with which many of us are familiar farther south.

## ◀ THE EGG

This is an unusual view of the Egg, a performing arts center in Empire State Plaza in downtown Albany. Known as the Plaza, this complex also includes state office buildings, a convention center, concourse, and museum. Completed in 1978 at a cost of more than $2 billion, it fulfilled Governor Rockefeller's dream of a center that would draw visitors to the city and give them a sense of pride in their state government.

## ▶ HUDSON RIVER SUNSET NEAR ATHENS

Founded in 1686, the Athens area was originally named Loonenburg. In 1778 the first ferry connecting Athens and Hudson began operation. Although the Rip Van Winkle Bridge opened in 1935, this ferry continued transporting people across the river until 1947.

◀ WATERFALL IN THE MIST,
PLATTE CLOVE PRESERVE

This scene reminds us that no other river
spawned a school of painting like the
Hudson River School. Inspired by vistas
such as this one, Thomas Cole, Frederic
Edwin Church, and Albert Bierstadt created
their masterpieces. The celebrities of their
day, they painted simple scenes in a natural
setting. This uniquely American school of
landscape art flourished during the late
1800s; however, after the turn of the century,
with the rise in popularity of photography,
its work fell out of favor. Thomas Cole, an
early environmentalist, desired progress,
yet also wanted to preserve the wilderness.
Even then, the Hudson River was being
threatened by pollution with the steamboat
era, which began with Fulton's Folly in
1807 at Clermont.

▶ KAATERSKILL FALLS,
CATSKILL PRESERVE

The sight that awed nineteenth-century
visitors to the Catskills perhaps more than
any other were these waterfalls, which also
inspired artists, poets, and photographers.
The falls are 260 feet high, 20 feet higher
than Niagara Falls.

## ◀ VERNOOYKILL CREEK

The creek is named for Cornelius Vernooy, one of the first settlers in the Rondout Valley in the early eighteenth century. He set up the first grist mill in the region, with machinery brought over from his native Holland.

## ▶ VIEW FROM SUGARLOAF MOUNTAIN

## ▲ STORMY DAY AT
## DEVIL'S KITCHEN

Platte Clove Preserve in Greene County
is filled with waterfalls, and an air of
mystery and magic, captured here.

## ▶ DEVIL'S ADVOCATE

This is Rich Romano, New Paltz resident,
a 46-year-old ice climbing expert. You
would never guess it from meeting him,
though. He's the nicest, laid back guy—you
just don't see any of that intensity.

Hardie and Rich have known one
another for more than 30 years. Whenever
Hardie has photographed him, Rich has
worn dark-colored clothes. For this particular shot, Hardie instructed him to wear
bright gear. "But my bright stuff isn't water-
proof," Rich said, explaining that the ice is
continually dripping. To set up the photo,
where this awesome, nearly vertical hillside
descends into a gorge, took close to twenty
minutes. Water was running into Rich's
clothes and boots, and by the time Hardie
began shooting, Rich was drenched. "I sacri-
ficed my comfort for art," he recalled,
amused at the memory.

When I remarked about the steepness
of the ice wall, Rich told me that this ven-
ture is not as difficult as it appears—all the
ice is climbable. "Ice is a fickle medium,"
he said. "One day it's hard, the next it's not,
it's always changing . . . one day you climb
an ice wall, the next day what you climbed
has disappeared."

## ◀ ESCARPMENT TRAIL, NORTH AND SOUTH LAKES

A renowned place for Hudson River School painters to set up their easels, this 24-mile-long historic trail reveals magnificent views laced with colorful history. In this area of the Catskills, there is an enormous diversity of plant species due to the varied soils—limestone and shale at the escarpment base, and a rocky acidic mix from broken-down conglomerate around the peaks. This photograph was taken from Sunset Rock. While the grand hotels are long gone, North and South Lakes, visible in the distance, have become popular tourist destinations.

## ▶ VIEW FROM THE RIP VAN WINKLE BRIDGE

Looking south on a crystal clear afternoon, the Hudson River appears to be strikingly blue and clean. A cantilevered bridge connecting Catskill and Hudson, the Rip Van Winkle span opened to traffic on July 2, 1935 and cost $2.5 million to build.

### ▶ OLANA STATE HISTORIC SITE

Frederic Edwin Church, a painter who captured the mystery and grandeur of nineteenth-century America, first gained acclaim for his vision of Niagara Falls in a painting that won a medal at the Paris International Exhibition in 1867. A few years later, Church and his wife, Isabel, returned to their farm in Hudson, New York, after traveling extensively in the Middle East and Europe. They built a 37-room Persian-style mansion and named it Olana, which means "our castle on high" in Arabic. Situated 460 feet above the river, with hand-painted tiles on the roof, it adds touches of pink and green to the sky.

Church referred to his style as "personal Persia." And inside this unique home, chock full of hand-carved, room-sized screens, richly colored rugs, delicate paintings, and decorative china, are dozens of Church's paintings. In fact, his studio is still set up as it was in his time, seemingly awaiting his entrance.

### ▶ FROZEN SUNSET, CLERMONT STATE PARK

"Light is the greatest stimulant; it is the fire of life."
—Thomas Cole

## ◄ CRUGER ISLAND SHORELINE

Now part of the mainland, this former island, once owned by Colonel John Church Cruger, has an interesting history. In the early 1840s Cruger was given several enormous Mayan sculptures and various artifacts by an explorer friend who often traveled to Mexico and Central America. The ruins were shipped via steamboat to Cruger's island country home in Dutchess County, where they adorned the grounds, complete with stone paths leading to a temple. Cruger took pride in showing off his treasures, especially during moonlight cruises. Ancient ruins were in vogue during this time; they often were the subject of local artist Thomas Cole's paintings. When the foliage thins, glimpses of the island may still be seen by river travelers. In 1919 the sculptures were bought by the American Museum of Natural History, and they may be seen there today.

## ► FLOWERING SERVICEBERRY TREE, THOMPSON POND NATURE PRESERVE

At the base of Stissing Mountain (Pine Plains, Dutchess County), Thompson Pond teems with wildlife and a fascinating variety of plants and trees.

◀ **KINGSTON–RHINECLIFF BRIDGE**

Opened to traffic on February 2, 1957, the bridge was designed by D. B. Steinman. The bridge is of the continuous deck design and has an overall length of 7,793 feet. Taken from Ulster Landing in Kingston, this photo is particularly eye-catching, with the black tree in the left foreground in contrast to the brightness of the other elements at a distance.

▶ **BLOODROOT FLOWERS WITH RAINDROPS, THOMPSON POND NATURE PRESERVE**

### ◄ POET'S WALK, RIVER ROAD, RED HOOK

Opened in June 1996, thanks to the Scenic Hudson Land Trust, this 120-acre park, with paths that meander through fields, over stone footbridges, and around arbors, offers wonderful views of the Hudson River, Catskill Mountains, and the Kingston–Rhinecliff Bridge at almost every turn.

Families would be isolated for weeks, and there was no electricity at the time.

The last residents departed in 1939, when the U.S. Coast Guard acquired the lighthouse. The old oil lamps were extinguished in 1965 and the lights were automated. The lighthouse gradually began to deteriorate, until 1990, when the Save the Esopus Lighthouse Commission was created to restore this historic structure.

▶ **ESOPUS ISLAND IN THE MIST, HUDSON RIVER NEAR ESOPUS**

▲ **MAID OF THE MEADOWS**

The area surrounding the Esopus Meadows Lighthouse in Ulster Park is exceedingly shallow; shoals and mud flats are dangerous for ships, and even small boats can easily run aground on the sharp reefs. The two-story wood framed lighthouse with clapboard exterior was built in 1839 on an artificial island, and is listed on the National Register of Historic Places. All lighthouses of similar design on the Hudson have long since disappeared.

Also known as Maid of the Meadows, the lighthouse cost $6,000 to build. Damaged by floods and ice in 1867, it was reconstructed in 1871.

Since the lighthouse is only accessible by boat, the seven rooms were designed for a family residence (the keeper, his wife and children). There was a kitchen, dining, and sitting room on the first floor with bedrooms upstairs. During the winter months, substantial amounts of ice often built up, preventing boats from docking.

## ◀ KINGSTON LIGHTHOUSE

Many Ulster County denizens, like myself, have a snapshot of the Kingston Lighthouse, perhaps tucked away in a pile of photos . . . and probably taken from a tour boat during that first summer living in the area. Why, I wonder, is this one such a standout? It's that tree! It seems to anchor the photograph, its blackness juxtaposed starkly against an array of colors in the background light. "Did you intentionally set up the photo that way?" I asked Hardie. "No, I had a gut feeling including the tree would make the composition just right," he replied, somewhat bemused by my question.

## ▶ OLD DUTCH CHURCH, KINGSTON

Many popular images of this church include a spring view with thousands of red tulips lining the church walks. This one, photographed near the historic Frederick J. Johnston Museum on Wall Street, focuses on the amazing spire, a Kingston landmark in the uptown historic district. Dating back to 1659, the Reformed Protestant Dutch Church has served the people of the area for more than three centuries. Governor DeWitt Clinton's gravesite is located in the surrounding churchyard.

### ◀ ASHOKAN RESERVOIR AT SUNSET

Ashokan is an Indian word that is believed to mean "the place of many fishes." The reservoir contains 40 miles of shoreline, with trout, walleye, and bass lurking beneath its waters. Perhaps the possibility of a meal intrigues these gulls gathering on the rocks.

### ▶ SNOW-LADEN SPRUCE TREES, SLIDE MOUNTAIN SUMMIT

Slide Mountain, elevation 4,180 feet, is the highest peak in the Catskills. The mountain is part of 47,500 acres of wilderness area in the northwestern corner of Ulster County. At the summit, a plaque commemorates naturalist John Burroughs, who once observed that "here the works of man dwindle." Those who reach the summit of Slide Mountain will surely agree.

## ◀ ▶ SUMMIT OF WITTENBERG MOUNTAIN

Wittenberg and Slide Mountains in Ulster County were favorites of naturalist John Burroughs (1837–1921). These views from the top of Wittenberg demonstrate why the British wanted to change the name of the Catskills (which sounded too Dutch to them) to the Blue Mountains.

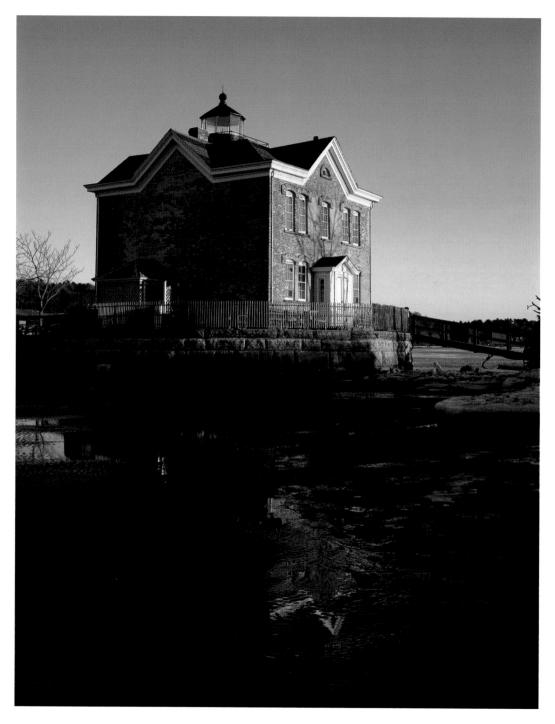

### ◀ SAUGERTIES LIGHTHOUSE WITH TIDAL REFLECTIONS

This is the only Hudson River lighthouse with its own bed and breakfast. That's right—visitors can stay overnight . . . something I did in June 1997, after walking out there on a rather rocky trail at low tide. The winds gently blew through the windows on all three sides of the upstairs bedroom where I slept. From the Light Tower, another floor higher, there is a spectacular view of the heavens at night, and, during daylight hours, the Hudson River with the Catskills looming in the background. Those views are to be enjoyed only if you are game for the rather tricky ascent up the steep stairs. . . . But it's well worth the physical challenge.

The first lighthouse here, built in 1838, when Saugerties was a major port with daily commerical and passenger transportation, was illuminated by five whale-oil lamps with parabolic reflectors. The current light was built in 1869, and sits on a massive circular stone base 60 feet in diameter. The foundation for the original lighthouse remains as a small island adjacent to the existing structure.

### ▶ SUNSET AT STURGEON POOL, RIFTON (ULSTER COUNTY)

## ◄ ▶ OPUS 40

Artist Harvey Fite's bluestone quarry in Saugerties was merely the source of material for his magnum opus, an enormous sculpture built in 1938. As work progressed, Fite realized that the steps and terraces he created as a backdrop for the sculpture had themselves become the focus. Naming the site Opus 40 because he believed it would take 40 years to complete, Fite embarked on the creation of a vast work that eventually would include 6 acres of steps, fountains, pools, and paths. Each of the thousands of bluestone pieces was hand-cut and fitted, and the 9-ton monolith centerpiece was lifted into place with a boom and winches.

This unusual environmental sculpture is now open to the public, and is occasionally used as a concert site. Fite, who worked as an actor and teacher, built a small museum on the premises to house the collection of quarryman's tools he used during the construction of Opus 40. Also on view is the array of artifacts he discovered on the site. A stop here offers a glimpse into a way of life long gone and rarely contemplated.

### ◀ PERRINE BRIDGE

This 154-foot-long covered bridge crossing the Wallkill River in Rifton was designed with a burr arch truss. The bridge was constructed in 1844 and restored in 1993; the builder is unknown. The bridge is easily accessible, a treat for pedestrians, but vehicular traffic is prohibited.

### ▶ AMERICAN SKYDIVER

Joe Richards, the owner of Skydive the Ranch in Gardiner, says the rush of adrenaline comes as you exit the airplane, just before you jump out and release the parachute, a feeling most of us will never choose to experience. Before going up, it's critical to check the wind direction and velocity. "That way you can gauge how to make it back to the airport," he explained. "I always do that . . . well, at least most of the time!"

## ◀ THE HIGH FALLS IN HIGH FALLS

The Delaware and Hudson Canal was closed in 1898, but in the early nineteenth century rivers thrived as commercial waterways. Where the rivers didn't intersect, canals were constructed, like the D&H (which connected the Delaware and Hudson Rivers), to transport cement and coal to market in New York City. In its heyday, the D&H ran 108 miles from Honesdale, Pennsylvania to Kingston, New York.

The lock-dominated village of High Falls still has the remains of several canal locks, all within walking distance of the main street. These falls, which give the town its name, provided the setting for the movie *Splendor in the Grass*. Film buffs may recall the base of these falls as the spot where Natalie Wood's character nearly drowns.

## ▶ STONE HOUSE WINDOW, NEW PALTZ

A detail of the Jean Hasbrouck House, a former store and tavern. One of the renowned Huguenot Street stone houses, it contains a massive brick chimney, the only one of its kind in the United States. In 1677, twelve Huguenot families purchased 40,000 acres of land from the

Esopus Indians and began the settlement referred to as "die Pfalz," after an area in their homeland, the Rhineland Palatinate. Fifteen years later, the original log huts were replaced by stone houses, several of which still stand today thanks to the efforts of the Huguenot Historical Society.

## ◀ STONE ARCH BRIDGE

This three-arched stone bridge, which spans Callicoon Creek in Sullivan County, is the only remaining one of its kind in America. Built in 1872 by two German stonemasons, the bridge was constructed from hand-cut local stone and is supported without an outer framework. Replacing an earlier wooden span that collapsed from the constant weight of wagonloads of lumber, the Stone Arch Bridge gained fame not only for its graceful design and unusual construction, but also for a bizarre murder that took place there in 1892. A local farmer, believing that his brother-in-law had put a hex on him, convinced his son that only the man's death could lift the curse. So his son carried out the murder, and dumped the body into the river. Today, visitors fish from the banks of the creek, picnic on shore, or stroll through the nine-acre park surrounding the bridge, most of them oblivious to the events that occurred where they stand.

## ▶ EVENING ROCKS, DELAWARE RIVER

## ◀ INTERIOR OF THE VANTRAN COVERED BRIDGE

Built in 1860, this covered bridge, a single-span town lattice truss with a laminated archway, crosses the Willowemac Creek. Located in a small park just northeast of the town of Livingston Manor, it is a local treasure, although not a hidden one. Route 17 can be seen from the bridge and the park.

## ▶ RED DAWN, TRAPPS FALL

The Trapps cliffs, a two-mile-long section of rock layers, appear as a straight line in the distance when driving west out of the village of New Paltz. The ridges of the Shawangunk Mountains were formed by erosion in the earth's crust, produced by plate movements. After millions of years of this process, the hard Shawangunk layers remain elevated above the terrain of softer shales and limestones, leaving those dramatic quartz cliffs looming over the valley below.

## ► LOST CITY MIST

"Lost City," bathed in morning mist, highlights the mystical ambience of the Shawangunks. Hardly anyone taking in the panorama from this vantage point would ever imagine that less than five miles away lies the bustling village of New Paltz. It is due to a melding of natural magic and the efforts of preservationists that this spectacular area retains its appearance from a time when people were not part of the landscape.

## ►► BLACK BIRCH IN THE MIST, UNDERCLIFF ROAD

Undercliff Road is remarkable for its dramatic overhanging cliffs and is one of the best walking paths in the Shawangunks. Built along the top of a mass of fallen boulders, its construction by the Smiley family of Mohonk involved enormous amounts of hand labor to move great blocks of stone and break apart large rocks into small ones to be used for support walls. A near-level road was completed in 1903, ideal for touring by horse and carriage back then, and perfect today for walking, cycling, and cross-country skiing.

## ◀ LAKE AWOSTING, MINNEWASKA STATE PARK

The largest of the five mountaintop lakes, 1.25 miles in length, Awosting was once called Long Pond.

## ▶ AWOSTING FALLS

A jewel of the Shawangunks, where the Peters Kill stream spills over a cliff of beautifully layered rocks, Awosting Falls is about a three-mile walk from the entrance to Minnewaska State Park.

◄ SUNSET PATH CARRIAGEWAY
IN AUTUMN MIST,
MINNEWASKA STATE PARK

## ◄◄ GERTRUDE'S NOSE TRAIL

This clifftop trail (approximately three miles long) revealing magnificent mountain vistas at almost every turn, is a popular hike among visitors to Minnewaska State Park. Undoubtedly, the dramatic views of Palmaghatt Ravine will make those who are afraid of heights a little queasy. The large boulders, which seem as though they were placed strategically along the trail, were deposited there by glaciers.

A great wedge-like mass of conglomerate, resembling a proboscis, juts out from the escarpment. Gertrude Bruyn, who was of Dutch descent and originally owned this land, did not have a large nose. The word "noes" is Dutch for promontory. Hence the Anglicized version of the name, Gertrude's Nose, implying the area was hers.

## ◄ ICE CAVES WITH SPRING FERNS, SAM'S POINT PRESERVE

A look inside any of the ice caves offers a glimpse of how erosion can be spectacularly beautiful. The geology of the Shawangunks is nowhere unfolded so dramatically as here.

### ◀ BOULDERS AT SAM'S POINT

Sam's Point, at 2,255 feet above sea level, was formed by glaciers that left behind an array of rocks after successive sheets of ice covered the region millions of years ago. In certain areas, these boulders seem to create peculiar patterns, as if some other-worldly force placed them exactly where they are. On a clear day, five states are visible from Sam's Point (New York, New Jersey, Pennsylvania, Connecticut, and Massachusetts). The place supposedly derived its name from a trapper named Sam who, fleeing a Native American war party, jumped over the cliffs and luckily landed in some trees.

Despite safety walls along the precipices, when walking along Sam's Point one feels precariously suspended over the sweeping valley below.

### ▲ VERKEERDER KILL FALLS

During the spring, the sight and sound of these spectacular falls cascading into pools 100 feet below mesmerizes onlookers with their deafening thunder. A rainbow may often be seen, intensifying this scenic wonder.

◀ **PINK MOUNTAIN LAUREL AT SAM'S POINT PRESERVE**

June is when the mountain laurel blooms in the Hudson Valley, a perfect time to hike and observe these stunning flowering shrubs.

▶ **BERRY BUSHES AT SAM'S POINT DWARF PINE RIDGE PRESERVE**

These eerie looking pine barrens, also referred to as the Badlands, near Verkeerder Kill Falls, are a gem of the Shawangunks.

◄ SUNFLOWERS, ULSTER
COUNTY

► MOHONK PRESERVE
This nature preserve (more than 5,000 acres)
is surrounded by 2,000 acres owned by the
Mohonk Mountain House.

◀ ROCK RIFT TALUS AND MIST,
MOHONK PRESERVE

◀ FROZEN MOUNTAIN
WINTERBERRIES AT MOHONK
PRESERVE

▶ AUTUMN VIEW OF
THE LAKE AND MOHONK
MOUNTAIN HOUSE

Mohonk Mountain House was built by the
Smiley family, nineteenth-century environ-
mentalists. The hotel remains family-owned,
and dedicated to preserving the natural
world. A National Historic Landmark, it
remains largely unchanged, enduring the
last century with timeless grace.

◄ THE GARDENS AT MOHONK
MOUNTAIN HOUSE

► PITCH PINE BUDS AMID
QUARTZ CONGLOMERATE
AT MOHONK PRESERVE

## ◀ FLOWERING APPLE TREES

The tower at Sky Top (visible in the background), the highest point along the Preserve's miles of trails (1,500 feet above sea level), was built in 1920 as a memorial to Albert Smiley, one of the founders of the hotel, which opened in 1870.

## ▶ RUSS RAFFA CLIMBING TRAPPS CLIFF

The Shawangunk Mountains are one of the most renowned rock climbing destinations in the world. Here Russ Raffa ascends the route "Directissima" at Trapps Cliff.

▲ RICH ROMANO WITH
AN UNUSUAL VIEW OF
THE SHAWANGUNKS.
Yes, he is the same person photographed
ice climbing. Here he tackles an overhang
on Trapps Cliff.

◀ ROCK CLIMBER BETWEEN
TWO ROCKS AND A HARD
PLACE
Morris Hershoff stems a corner in the
Gunks.

## ▶ REFLECTIONS OF AUTUMN AT DUCK POND

Duck Pond, formed in 1908 by damming the Kleine Kill stream, is 600 feet in elevation. It's a beautiful place to stop and marvel at the fall colors.

◀◀ SAUCER MAGNOLIA
BLOSSOMS

◀ TABLE ROCKS SUNSET

Table Rocks, a huge outcropping of
conglomerate, is bordered by dramatic
cliffs. Here its enormous fissure is
captured highlighted by the setting sun.

### ◀ AUTUMN FLORA

"The time of the falling of leaves has come again. Once more in our morning walk we tread upon carpets of gold and crimson, of brown and bronze, woven by the winds or the rains out of these delicate textures while we slept. How beautifully the leaves grow old. How full of light and color are their last days!"

—John Burroughs,
*John Burroughs' America*

### ▶ AUTUMN EVENING, BONTICOU CRAG SUMMIT

The spectacular views from Bonticou Crag Summit include the Catskills to the northwest, Stissing Mountain (Dutchess County) to the northeast, and the Hudson Highlands to the southeast.

## MID-HUDSON BRIDGE

Opened to traffic on August 25, 1930, replacing a long-operating ferry line, the Mid-Hudson Bridge is 3,000 feet long. The construction cost for this span, joining Highland with the city of Poughkeepsie, was $5.89 million. The majestic towers, particularly striking at night, are the masterpiece of Ralph Modjeski (1861–1940), born in Cracow, Poland, and the leading bridge designer of his day.

## ► WING'S CASTLE

This unique castle-in-progress, complete with moat, has been under construction for more than 25 years. Builder/actor/home-owner Peter Wing and his wife, Toni, have fashioned an antique ship as a balcony. They can bathe in a cauldron tub, complete with terra cotta fountain. The Wings use salvaged materials from antique buildings to create what they call a recycled-Americana-style home, crammed full of bric-a-brac and collectibles. Carousel horses and suits of armor vie for space with stained-glass windows and military weapons. Right out of a fairy tale, it is a glorious example of the creativity of some Hudson Valley residents.

## ◀ INNISFREE GARDENS, MILLBROOK

Inspired by the Eastern cup garden, these individual "garden pictures" draw attention to a particular object, setting it apart by establishing an enclosure around it. Following the tradition of Asian artists, garden founder Walter Beck used natural formations, as well as terraces, walls, and paths, to keep specific areas in "tension," believing that moving rocks or plants only an inch or so would destroy the effect.

## ▶ VANDERBILT EVENING

The Vanderbilt Mansion, bathed in evening light, is testament to an era long gone, yet is surrounded by vistas largely unchanged over the centuries. Walk the grounds just before an autumn sunset and imagine how Frederick Vanderbilt and his family must have enjoyed living here during the spring and fall. This imposing Beaux Arts mansion, constructed at a cost of $660,000, is part of a 100-mile stretch of palatial Gilded Age homes built during the nineteenth century along the banks of the Hudson River. The captains of industry who built these mansions played the role of gentleman farmer for part of the year but remained entrenched in a rigid class society in both city and country venues.

## ◀ HUDSON RIVER ICE FLOES NEAR NORRIE STATE PARK

Unlike the upper part of the river, the lower Hudson River rarely freezes solid. The headwaters of the Hudson are upstate and the water coming down the river is colder and mostly fresh, with a freezing point of 32 degrees. The lower Hudson is warmer, being farther south, and contains more salt water, which freezes at about 28–30 degrees.

## ▶ BANNERMAN'S ISLAND SUNSET

Pollepel Island, approximately 7 acres of rock near Cornwall·on·Hudson, is home to the ruins of Bannerman's Castle. The name of the island could be derived from *potlepel*, the Dutch word for pot ladle. Ship passengers who "ladled" too much liquor were put off at Pollepel to sober up, and were later picked up on the boat's return trip. Another possibility is that the name comes from an eighteenth·century woman, Polly Pell, who was rescued from the river during the winter and brought to the island. It became known as Bannerman's Island in the late nineteenth century, when a munitions merchant of the same name bought the island for a place to store weapons and ammunition he bought at government auctions. Frank Bannerman designed the building in the style of old Scottish castles and lived there with his wife in baronial splendor. In 1967 the family sold the castle to New York State. On the night of August 8, 1969, a fire of unknown origin destroyed all the buildings. The castle is now under the aegis of the Bannerman Castle Trust, which intends to eventually open the island to the public.

## ▲ VIEW OF CONSTITUTION MARSH FROM BOSCOBEL

More than 200 species of birds have been observed in this brackish marsh off Constitution Island. Manhattan lawyer Henry Warner bought the island in 1836 and lived here with his two daughters, who never married and both became well·respected authors. In 1908 the island was given to West Point, and may be reached only by boat, kayak or canoe.

◄ BANNERMAN'S ISLAND
PANORAMA

► BANNERMAN'S ISLAND
WITH PASSING TUGBOAT

◀ VIEW FROM LITTLE STONY
POINT, HUDSON HIGHLANDS
STATE PARK

◀ TROPHY POINT BATTLE
MONUMENT, WEST POINT
This enormous monument, designed by
Stanford White, commemorates those who
lost their lives in battle during the Civil
War. Looking north from this unusual
vantage point affords dramatic views of
the Hudson River.

## ► BREAKNECK VIEWS

The Hudson Highlands is where the
Appalachian Mountains once made a
solid wall of granite where the river now
flows. Glaciers helped the river to force a
passage through them. This is one of the
few places in the thousand-mile-long
Appalachian chain that is breached by a
stream at sea level. These wildly beautiful
peaks and valleys were a place of sudden
storms and treacherous winds, where the
mountains were natural fortresses and the
valleys were traps, areas where armies could
be ambushed.

During the Revolutionary War, no
location on the continent was of more
importance to both the British and
American military than the Highlands.
This was the place where the Hudson
River, hemmed in and narrowed by the
mountains, would force a fleet into single
file, where it would be at the mercy of a
few well-placed cannon from above. This
is where a chain was stretched across the
river to ensnare the enemy. This is where
the river is at its deepest, 200 feet to the
bottom. And this is why West Point
became what it is where it is.

PAGE 98-99 **STORM KING
AND BREAKNECK RIDGE
FROM THE BATTLE
MONUMENT**

◀ ICE FLOE SUNSET
AND STORM KING

▼ LAKE KANAWAUKEE
Many names of the beautiful lakes in
Harriman State Park, like this one, are not
derived from the dialect of the Delaware

Indians who once lived in the area.
However, Kanawaukee is an actual
Indian word, and reminds us who
originally inhabited our region.

► FIELD OF COLOR,
HARRIMAN STATE PARK

►► IONA MARSH IN WINTER

Iona Island, a winter sanctuary for the bald eagle, is located at the narrows of the Hudson, just south of the Bear Mountain Bridge. Few travelers driving along Route 9W stop to explore this unusal part of the Palisades Interstate Park System, perhaps because the sign for Iona Island is easy to miss. This photograph was taken from the marsh-bordered causeway that links the island to the shore. Don't forget the binoculars!

◄ ◄ APPROACHING STORM
WITH A VIEW OF IONA ISLAND

◄ BEAR MOUNTAIN BRIDGE
When completed in 1924, this was the
world's longest suspension span at 2,258
feet in length. Privately built at a cost of
$5 million, the Bear Mountain Bridge was
designed by Howard Baird of New York
City, and acquired by the state of New
York for $2.3 million in 1940. It links
Putnam and Westchester Counties on the
east side of the Hudson with Orange and
Rockland Counties on the west side.

The subject of a great deal of curiosity—
and folklore—is a jutting rock formation at
the east end of the bridge called Anthony's
Nose. According to Washington Irving,
in the early seventeenth century, Dutch
Governor Peter Stuyvesant sailed up the
river to survey his lands. Accompanying
him was Anthony Van Corlear, who had
an amazingly distinctive nose. Stuyvesant
decided his friend's proboscis was reminis-
cent of the prominent headland where
the bridge is today, hence the name.

### ◄ HOOK MOUNTAIN

Taken from the Hudson River, near the village of Nyack (Rockland County), this photograph shows Hook Mountain in all its glory. Once referred to by the Dutch as Verdrietige (tedious headland), because the winds could change so quickly in this area and leave a boat adrift, the area was favored as a campground by Native Americans due to its wealth of oysters, which are, unfortunately, long gone.

### ► TAPPAN ZEE BRIDGE

Tappan is the Indian word for "cold spring," and zee is Dutch for sea. Built in 1955, this is one of the largest bridges in America, with a length of 15,764 feet (nearly 3 miles). Viewing the Tappan Zee from this unusal vantage point, you might not imagine that more than 27 acres of pavement were used on the road area. Eight concrete caissons supported on steel piles driven into rock serve as underwater foundations to support most of the structure's dead weight. The largest caisson weighs 15,000 tons. They were made in Haverstraw and floated down the river into place. The bridge connects Rockland and Westchester Counties.

◄ CROTON DAM

The Croton Dam, also known as the
Cornell Dam, is more than 200 feet high.
The Croton River drains an area of about
350 square miles. Close to Manhattan, it
became the place to build reservoirs. A dam
was constructed in 1837, and work began
on a stone aqueduct to New York City. The
dam was swept away by a flood in 1841, but
was quickly rebuilt. Between 1884 and 1890
the system was enlarged to a total capacity
of 100 million gallons per day. The 38-mile-
long aqueduct dating back to 1842 is out
of use, but the reservoirs continue to
contribute their waters to the Catskill
and Delaware Aqueduct systems.

► MOSSY HEMLOCK ROOTS
IN THE MONTE GLORIA AREA
OF THE MIANUS RIVER GORGE
PRESERVE

◀ BOULDERS IN THE
MIANUS RIVER

The Mianus River Gorge Preserve is
named after Chief Mayano of the
Wappinger tribe, whose name in the
Indian language means "he who gathers
together." The area, located in the town
of Bedford, is one of the best places to hike
in Westchester County. This magical
photograph was taken on a rainy day in
the Rockwell Breach area of the preserve.

## ◄ PHILIPSBURG MANOR

This patrician homestead, founded in the seventeenth century by Frederick Philipse, an immigrant Dutch carpenter, was once the center of a 50,000-acre estate. The manor thrived as part of a bustling commercial empire that included milling and trading businesses. For almost a century, members of the Philipse family were respected colonists, but during the Revolutionary War they fled to England as Loyalists, and their landholdings were broken up. On a visit to this state historic site, you may journey back in time by watching the water-powered mill grind cornmeal, exactly as it did more than 300 years ago.

## ► THE PALISADES AT STATE LINE LOOKOUT

The rock formations known as the Palisades run from Bayonne, New Jersey to Pomona, New York, for about 48 miles. The highest point, Indian Head, is 522 feet and is opposite Hastings-on-Hudson. Named for their similarity in appearance to wooden palisaded fortifications, these towering cliffs along the western shore of the Hudson River near the border between New York and New Jersey are particularly striking amid the fall colors.

◀ NIGHT VIEW OF GEORGE
WASHINGTON BRIDGE
WITH MANHATTAN SKYLINE

Upon completion (the upper deck was
opened to traffic in 1931, and the lower deck
in 1962), the George Washington Bridge
became the world's only 14-lane suspension
bridge. Space was allotted at the top of its
two towers for restaurants and observation
decks, to be accessed by elevators from the
sidewalks on either side of the upper level,
but they were never built. Night views of the
bridge are still magical from many other
vantage points.

▶ STATUE OF LIBERTY,
NEW YORK HARBOR

◄ NEW YORK CITY SKYLINE
This photograph was taken in 2000
from Liberty State Park in New Jersey.

# DIRECTIONS: IF YOU WANT TO GO

Driving directions are given from the south heading north.

ADIRONDACK VIEWS FROM MOUNT MARCY, ADIRONDACK PRESERVE *(page 13)*
Take the New York State Thruway north to exit 24. After paying the toll, follow signs to 1N (The Northway). Get off at exit 30, and follow Route 73 north toward Lake Placid. Heart Lake Road is unmarked, but it begins 11.2 miles west of Keene and 3.2 miles east of Lake Placid off Route 73. Follow Heart Lake Road south to the end where there is a visitor center, lodge, and campground run by the Adirondack Mountain Club. The trailhead for Mount Marcy and Lake Tear of the Clouds is at the end of Heart Lake Road. Note that the hike to the lake from this point is nearly 19 miles round-trip.

INDIAN LAKE SUNRISE *(page 14)*
Take the New York State Thruway north. Get off the Thruway at Exit 24 in Albany and follow signs to Route 90 West after paying the toll. Take exit 27 off Route 90. Follow Route 30 North off the exit for approximately 65 miles. Route 30 follows the western shore of Indian Lake, where this photograph was taken.

BLUE LEDGE TRAIL, ADIRONDACK PRESERVE *(page 15)*
Take the New York State Thruway north to exit 24. After paying the

toll, follow signs to 1N (The Northway). Get off at exit 23 and follow Route 9 North to Route 28 (in North Creek), about 20 miles from the exit. Take Route 28N through Minerva (9.4 miles from the intersection of Routes 28 & 28N in North Creek). Turn left onto North Woods Club Road. You will cross a one-lane bridge after 3.8 miles. Go another 3 miles to the trailhead on the eastern edge of Huntley Pond. The trail is 5 miles round-trip.

THE EGG, ALBANY *(page 16)*
Take the New York State Thruway north to Albany (exit 23). After paying the toll, you will be on 787. Exit at Empire State Plaza. The exit will take you right past the parking garage. Follow signs for North or South parking which will leave you a short walk away.

HUDSON RIVER SUNSET NEAR ATHENS *(page 17)*
Take the New York State Thruway to exit 21, Catskill. After paying the toll, make a left turn; about ½ mile up the road, make another left turn, following signs to the Rip Van Winkle Bridge. At the traffic light, located just before the approach to the bridge, make a left, and continue 4 miles to Athens. Make a right turn down Second Street and you will be at the riverfront.

WATERFALL IN THE MIST, PLATTE CLOVE PRESERVE *(page 18)* and STORMY DAY AT DEVIL'S KITCHEN, PLATTE CLOVE PRESERVE *(page 22)*
Take the New York State Thruway north to exit 20 (Saugerties). Make a left off the exit, staying to the right. A few hundred feet in front of you is the right turn for Route 32. Stay on this road, bearing to the left when it forks into 32A, through Palenville, until you come to a traffic light and the place where you turn left onto Route 23A. Continue up the mountain road through Haines Falls and Tannersville. The next major road on the left is Bloomer Road (there is a lumber company there). Turn left. Bloomer Road eventually turns into Platte Clove Road. Continue until you see signs for Platte Clove Preserve; the parking area is on the right side of the road.

KAATERSKILL FALLS *(page 19)*
There are a few ways to reach the falls, but one of the most scenic routes is to take the New York State Thruway to exit 20 (Saugerties). Make a left at the light after paying the toll, then bear to the right onto Route 32. Follow for several miles

until the road splits to 32A; bear left and continue on 32. You will come to a traffic light in Palenville. Make a left onto Route 23A, heading toward Hunter. You will soon enter the Catskill Preserve. A twisting, turning road leads up into the mountains, and the falls are visible on the right at a hairpin turn. It is best to continue on toward North Lake and park there if you want to hike in, although people do park on the left side of the road in a small parking area, just after passing the falls.

### VERNOOYKILL CREEK
*(page 20)*
Take the New York State Thruway to exit 19 (Kingston). Make a right after paying the toll onto Route 28 West. After the traffic light, make a right onto Route 209 South toward Ellenville. At the traffic light in Kerhonkson make a right onto Clay Hill Road (unmarked). After a few miles you will come to a stop sign at the junction of Pataukunk Road (also known as County Route 3). Turn left onto Route 3 and make another left just after this turn onto Cherrytown Road. After about 4 miles is Baker Road. Continue on Cherrytown Road and make a left onto Upper Cherrytown Road, just after crossing a small brook. The trailhead is about 3 miles from this point, on the left side of the road (parking is on the right). The round-trip hike will take about two hours and is approximately 3½ miles.

### VIEW FROM SUGARLOAF
MOUNTAIN *(page 21)*
Take the New York State Thruway north to exit 20 (Saugerties). Make a left

off the exit, staying to the right. A few hundred feet in front of you is the right turn for Route 32. Stay on this road, bearing to the left when it forks into 32A, through Palenville, until you come to a traffic light and the place where you turn left onto Route 23A. Take Route 23A west through the village of Tannersville and make a left onto Bloomer Road. Go for about 2 miles to Elka Park Road and make a right. Bear left at the first fork in the road, and left again at the second fork, passing Mink Hollow Road on your right. Look for the trailhead sign and parking area on the right, about one mile past Mink Hollow Road. Follow Pequoy Notch Trail to the notch, about 1½ miles. Take the right trail up the eastern shoulder of Sugarloaf Mountain; look for the open ledges to the left of the trail.

### DEVIL'S ADVOCATE *(page 23)* and ESCARPMENT TRAIL, NORTH AND SOUTH LAKES *(page 24)*
Take the New York State Thruway to exit 20 (Saugerties). Make a left at the light after paying the toll, then bear to the right onto Route 32. Follow for several miles until the road splits to 32A; bear left and continue on 32. You will come to a traffic light in Palenville. Make a left onto Route 23A, heading toward Hunter. You will soon enter the Catskill Preserve. Continue on Route 23A past the Kaaterskill Falls parking area and take the first right turn, North Lake Road, going toward North Lake. Continue on for approximately 4 miles until the road ends. Turn right onto

Schutt Road, just before the entrance to the North/South Lake campground. There is a parking area here. Follow the blue-marked trail which is the Escarpment Trail.

### VIEW FROM THE RIP VAN WINKLE BRIDGE *(page 25)*
There are several ways to get to this bridge, depending on where you are coming from. On the east side of the river, Route 9G takes you from Poughkeepsie up to the bridge. On the west side of the river, take the New York State Thruway north to exit 21. Make a left off the exit and follow signs to the bridge which is only a few miles away. You can also get onto Route 9W and head north (or south if you are coming from the Albany area). This route takes you through many towns and villages and can often be much slower going.

### OLANA STATE HISTORIC SITE *(page 26)*
Olana is located in Columbia County, just south of Hudson and the Rip Van Winkle Bridge; the entrance is on Route 9G. If you cross the bridge, make a right turn onto 9G South and the sign is about ½ mile away, on the left.

### FROZEN SUNSET, CLERMONT STATE PARK *(page 27)*
After crossing the Kingston–Rhinecliff Bridge heading east from Ulster County, make a left turn at the second traffic light onto Route 9G North heading

toward Hudson. Just after you enter Columbia County, there will be a sign for Clermont, directing you to make a left turn into the state park. Follow this road for approximately 1 mile and look for the entrance sign on the right. This short road takes you down to the park and the river.

CRUGER ISLAND SHORELINE
(page 28)
Cross the Kingston–Rhinecliff Bridge heading east on Route 199. At the first traffic light, make a left turn onto County Route 103, one of the most scenic drives in the Hudson Valley. Follow Route 103 (River Road) several miles. Continue on through Annandale and then follow signs to the Bard College campus. When a large stone gatehouse appears in front of you, follow the road around to the right; on the left is Cruger Road, which goes down to the island.

FLOWERING SERVICEBERRY TREE (page 29) and BLOODROOT FLOWERS WITH RAINDROPS (page 31) Take Route 9 North into the village of Red Hook. Make a right onto Route 199 and follow to the town of Pine Plains. (You could also head north on the New York State Thruway, take exit 19, and follow 209 north across the Kingston–Rhinecliff Bridge, which becomes 199 East into Pine Plains.) The pond is located before the trailhead for Stissing Mountain, just outside the town of Pine Plains. At the intersection of Routes 82 and 199,

drive south for about ½ mile on Route 82. Make a right turn onto Lake Road, go across a causeway, and after another 1.6 miles, you will see the entrance to the sanctuary on the left.

KINGSTON–RHINECLIFF BRIDGE (page 30)
Take the New York State Thruway to exit 19. After the toll area, bear to the right heading west on Route 28. Go through the traffic light and just after that, take the exit (the sign reads Rhinecliff Bridge Route 209 North). The bridge is 4 miles ahead. If you are on the east side of the river, proceed north toward the Rhinebeck/Red Hook area (take Route 9, Route 9G or the Taconic Parkway). At the junction of Routes 9 and 9G, follow the signs for the bridge, a few miles north on Route 9G.

POET'S WALK, RIVER ROAD, RED HOOK (pages 32–33)
Cross the Kingston–Rhinecliff Bridge heading east (Route 209 North off the New York State Thruway at exit 19). Route 209 becomes Route 199 in Dutchess County. At the first traffic light make a left turn onto River Road. Approximately a mile down the road on the left is the entrance to the Poet's Walk, open daily from dawn to dusk. There is ample parking.

MAID OF THE MEADOWS, ULSTER PARK (page 34)
Take the New York State Thruway to exit 18 (New Paltz). Make a right turn at

the light off the exit (Route 299). Where 299 ends after 6 miles at a light, make a left turn onto Route 9W North. Look for the sign for Ulster Park (there will be a Dutch Reformed Church on the left) and not far after that point, is River Road (County Route 24) on the right. Turn here. Follow down to the riverfront and you will see Esopus Meadows on the right, as well as the lighthouse.

ESOPUS ISLAND IN THE MIST (page 35)
From exit 18 of the New York State Thruway, make a right onto 299 East. At the end of 299, turn left onto Route 9W North. About ¼ mile after the BOCES school on the right, before the town of Port Ewen, is River Road. Make a right and continue for 2½ miles. On the left side of River Road you will see Esopus Meadows Park. Although this photo was taken from a boat, there are fine views of the island from the park. If you have the time, take the ½-mile trail along the river; it's perfect for a short walk. There is a bench at the end of the trail, and the lighthouse and Esopus Island are visible the entire way.

KINGSTON LIGHTHOUSE (page 36)
Take the New York State Thruway to exit 19 (Kingston). Follow the roundabout to Route 587, and make a right turn. Continue straight through the traffic light and cross the road (this is where 587 ends and Broadway begins). Go to the end of Broadway, bearing left at the light after the entrance to 9W. This is the Rondout waterfront district of Kingston. There is a pocket park (Kingston Point Park) and maritime

museum at the foot of Broadway. From May through October, a few tour boats dock here. All of them pass by the lighthouse.

## OLD DUTCH CHURCH, KINGSTON *(page 37)*

Take the New York State Thruway to exit 19, Kingston. After paying the toll, enter the roundabout and get off at the second right (Washington Avenue). At the third traffic light, make a left turn onto North Front Street. Go through the next light, and make a right turn onto Fair Street. Continue until you get to another light at the junction of Main Street. On your right is the Old Dutch Church and cemetery.

## THE ASHOKAN RESERVOIR AT SUNSET *(page 38)*

While there are several ways to get to the reservoir, the following directions lead to the area known as the aqueduct, which is closed to traffic and where one can walk, roller blade, or run. Take the New York State Thruway to exit 19 (Kingston). After paying the toll, make the first right turn and follow signs to Route 28 West. Go approximately 15 miles to the town of Shokan. Make a left onto Reservoir Road. Follow until you cross a bridge over the reservoir and come to a T intersection. Make a left. Soon after, the road forks, make another left turn. At the yield sign, go left once again. About 2 miles up the road on the left is an unmarked road that leads to a parking area and the aqueduct.

## SNOW-LADEN SPRUCE TREES, SLIDE MOUNTAIN SUMMIT *(page 39)*

Take the New York State Thruway north to exit 19 (Kingston). Follow the signs off the roundabout for Route 28 West. Continue on Route 28 West past Phoenicia, to the town of Big Indian. Make a left on Big Indian Road. Trailhead parking is up the road about 10 miles on the left. The distance to the summit is 6½ miles round-trip.

## SUMMIT OF WITTENBERG MOUNTAIN *(pages 40 and 41)*

Take the New York State Thruway north to exit 19 (Kingston). Follow the signs off the roundabout for Route 28 West. Continue past Phoenicia. Just after the exit for the town, make a left onto Woodland Valley Road. The trailhead for Wittenberg Mountain is at the end of this road. There is a campground and parking area on the right. This is a very rugged hike.

## SAUGERTIES LIGHTHOUSE WITH TIDAL REFLECTIONS *(page 42)*

Take the New York State Thruway north to exit 20 (Saugerties). Make a right at the light after paying the toll, onto Route 212, which takes you through town. Follow Main Street to Route 9W North, as you leave Saugerties, heading toward Catskill. About a

mile outside of town is Mynderse Street. Make a right turn and continue along this road, which turns into Lighthouse Drive. Near the end of the road is a parking area. The 10-minute walk to the lighthouse should not be made at high tide. Call 845-247-0656 for tide schedule, or check the lighthouse web site (www.saugertieslighthouse.com) to find out when high tide will be on the day of your visit.

## SUNSET AT STURGEON POOL, RIFTON *(page 43)*

The pool is located about midway between Kingston and New Paltz, off Route 32 in Rifton. If you are coming from either town, follow signs to Route 32. Heading south from Kingston on Route 32, pass the turn for Rosendale, and cross a small bridge, then turn left onto Route 213. (If you are coming north from New Paltz, the sign for Rifton will be on your right off Route 32.) Continue along Route 213 through Rifton, and after about a mile you will see Sturgeon Pool on the left side of the road.

## OPUS 40, SAUGERTIES *(pages 44–45)*

Take the New York State Thruway north to exit 19. Make the first right turn off the roundabout onto Route 28 West. Follow signs to Woodstock, making a right turn onto Route 375. Route 375 ends at the junction of Route 212; make a right onto Route 212, heading toward Saugerties. About 3 miles along, make a right onto Glasco

Turnpike, a major intersection. After a few miles, the road forks and there will be a sign indicating a left turn to Opus 40. Less than a few hundred feet ahead, on the left, is Fite Road. Turn left, go to the end of the road, and park. Opus 40 is a short walk away.

PERRINE BRIDGE, RIFTON (*page 46*)

This covered bridge is located about midway between Kingston and New Paltz, off Route 32 in Rifton. If you are coming from either town, follow signs to Route 32. Heading south from Kingston, pass the turn for Rosendale, cross a small bridge, and turn left onto Route 213. The covered bridge is located on the left, and is visible from the road. If you are coming north from New Paltz, the sign for Rifton will be on your right off Route 32.

AMERICAN SKYDIVER, SKYDIVE THE RANCH, GARDINER (*page 47*)

Take the New York State Thruway to exit 18 (New Paltz). Make a left at the traffic light off the exit onto Route 299. The town of Gardiner is just south of New Paltz. The junction of Route 208 is well-signed. You will make a left and follow Route 208 south from town to the junction of 44/55. Make a right turn into town. Pass the Gardiner post office, where the road veers sharply to the left. Bear right, go about one mile; you will see a sign for the entrance to Skydive the Ranch.

THE HIGH FALLS IN HIGH FALLS (*page 48*)

Take the New York State Thruway to exit 19. After paying the toll, bear to the right onto Route 28 West. Go through the traffic light and stay to the right. Take the exit just after the light (the sign says Ellenville Route 209 South). Go approximately 8 miles into the town of Stone Ridge, and at the second traffic light, you will see the junction of Route 213 East. Make a left turn onto Route 213. After the next traffic light you cross a small bridge and enter the town of High Falls. If you look to the left as you cross the bridge you may be able to see the "high falls." (If you are coming from New Paltz, follow Route 299 East through town, cross a small bridge, and take the first right, Springtown Road. Follow signs to Mohonk Mountain House and take Mountain Rest Road past the hotel entrance. At the end of the road, make a left turn and the falls will be on your right.)

STONE HOUSE WINDOW, NEW PALTZ (*page 49*)

Take the New York State Thruway to exit 18 (New Paltz). Make a left at the traffic light after the toll booth onto Route 299 East. Just after leaving town, before the small bridge, make a right turn and you will soon see the stone houses. They are open for tours from late May through October.

STONE ARCH BRIDGE (*page 50*)

From the New York State Thruway, take Route 17 West to the Liberty exit and pick up Route 52 West. In Kenoza Lake you will see a sign for the entrance to the Stone Arch Bridge Historical Park.

EVENING ROCKS, DELAWARE RIVER (*page 51*)

The Delaware River virtually forms the border of New York State and Pennsylvania along the western side of Sullivan County. The easiest way to reach the river from the south is to follow Route 17 West to the Liberty exit. Here pick up Route 52 West and take it to the end, where it intersects with Route 97, in Narrowsburg (about midway down the river). This photograph was taken in that area.

INTERIOR OF THE VANTRAN COVERED BRIDGE (*page 52*)

Take Route 17 West, past Liberty to the Livingston Manor exit. The bridge is located just northeast of the town of Livingston Manor. In fact, it is so close to Route 17, the highway is visible from the bridge.

FALL MIST, SKYTOP (*page 10*) and RED DAWN and TRAPPS FALL (*page 53*)

Take the New York State Thruway to exit 18 (New Paltz). Make a left at the light after paying the toll (Route 299 West). Continue through town. After the Water Street market on your left, cross a small bridge and take the first right onto Springtown Road. After a mile, the road forks. Bear to the left. At the next stop sign, you will see Butterville Road. Turn left onto it. As you continue, Skytop will appear, as it does in this photograph. To view Trapps Fall, follow directions to Mohonk Preserve Visitors Center (below) and inquire within about finding the trail to Undercliff Road.

 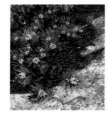

MOHONK PRESERVE, *pages 54–55, 67–70, 73–83:*

To reach Mohonk Preserve, take the New York State Thruway to exit 18 (New Paltz). Make a left at the light after paying the toll onto Route 299 West and continue through town. After the Water Street market on your left, you will cross a small bridge. Continue for several miles until 299

ends and make a right onto Route 44/55 West. The parking area and visitors center for the Mohonk Preserve is a couple of miles up the road on the right and is well signed.

LAKE AWOSTING (*page 56*), AWOSTING FALLS (*page 57*), SUNSET PATH CARRIAGEWAY IN AUTUMN MIST (*pages 58–59*), and GERTRUDE'S NOSE TRAIL (*page 60*), MINNEWASKA STATE PARK:

To reach Minnewaska State Park, take the New York State Thruway north to exit 18 (New Paltz). Make a left at the light after the toll booth onto 299 West and proceed through town for several miles until 299 ends at the junction of Routes 44/55. Make a right onto 44/55 West. The sign for the entrance to the park is on the left, about 4.4 miles up this mountain road.

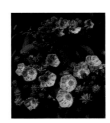

ICE CAVES WITH SPRING FERNS *(page 61)*, BOULDERS AT SAM'S POINT *(page 62)*, VERKEERDER KILL FALLS *(page 63)*, PINK MOUNTAIN LAUREL, *(page 64)*, BERRY BUSHES *(page 65)*

The entrance to Sam's Point Dwarf Pine Ridge Preserve is from the village of Cragsmoor, just out-side Ellenville. Take the New York State Thruway north to exit 19 (Kingston). After paying the toll, make the first right onto Route 28 West, and after the first light stay right, exiting at Route 209/Ellenville. It is about 25 miles to Ellenville, where you will see the junction of Route 52. Turn left here onto Route 52 East, and go for 3 miles. Make a left toward Cragsmoor. Pass the library on the left and at the post office, make a right turn. There is a sign for the preserve, and a parking area a little further up the road.

AUTUMN VIEW OF THE LAKE AND MOHONK MOUNTAIN HOUSE *(page 71) and* THE GARDENS AT MOHONK MOUNTAIN HOUSE *(page 72)*

Take the New York State Thruway to exit 18 (New Paltz). Make a left turn at the light off the exit onto Route 299 West. After passing through town and crossing a small bridge, immediately on the right is Springtown Road. Turn here. When the road forks, bear to the left. After about 4 miles, you will see the hotel entrance on the left.

NIGHT VIEWS, MID-HUDSON BRIDGE *(page 84)*

Follow Route 9 North and watch for signs to the bridge, which connects Highland and Poughkeepsie. If you are com-ing from Ulster County, Route 9W leads to the bridge, no matter which direction you are travel-ing in.

WING'S CASTLE, MILLBROOK *(page 85)*

Peter Wing's house is located five miles north of Millbrook, on Bangall Road, ½ mile north of Route 57 (adjacent to the Millbrook Winery). The castle is open May through October, Wednesday through Sunday, noon–4:30 PM; Labor Day through Christmas season, weekends only. Call 845-677-9085 for detailed directions and group tours.

INNISFREE GARDENS, MILLBROOK *(page 86)*

Take the Taconic Parkway north to the Route 44/Poughkeepsie exit. Head toward the town of Millbrook. Approximately one mile off Route 44, make a right onto Tyrell Road. You will see the parking area for the gar-dens ahead. Open May through October, Wednesday through Sunday, closed Monday and Tuesday. Call 845-677-8000 for hours.

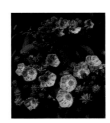

VANDERBILT EVENING, HYDE PARK *(page 87)*

The Vanderbilt Mansion is located off Route 9 at the northern end of the town of Hyde Park. The entrance is well signed.

HUDSON RIVER ICE FLOES NEAR NORRIE STATE PARK *(page 88–89)*

Take Route 9 North from Hyde Park, head-ing past the Vanderbilt Mansion. A few miles out-side Hyde Park you will enter Staatsburg. Make a left turn onto Old Post Road. You will then see signs for Norrie State Park and Norrie Environ-mental Center on the left.

VIEW OF CONSTITUTION MARSH FROM BOSCOBEL *(page 90)*

Follow Route 9 North to Peekskill. Just after the exit for the city, follow signs to the bridge and make a left, crossing a small bridge over Annsville Creek into a traffic circle. Follow signs in the traffic circle

to the Bear Mountain Bridge. On the east side of the bridge head north on Route 9D. The entrance to Boscobel, a State Historic Site, is on the left in the town of Garrison, and is well signed.

BANNERMAN'S ISLAND SUNSET *(page 91)*, BANNERMAN'S ISLAND PANORAMA *(page 92)*, and BANNERMAN'S ISLAND WITH PASSING TUGBOAT *(page 93)*

Take Route 9 North to the junction of Route 301. Make a left onto 301 into the village of Cold Spring. As you enter town, you will see Route 9D ahead of you. Continue on Route 9D. The sunset photograph was taken just outside town. There is a small parking area located off the road.

VIEW FROM LITTLE STONY POINT (HUDSON HIGHLANDS STATE PARK) *(page 94)*

See above directions for Bannerman's Island. There is trailhead parking, and a bridge across the railroad tracks to the river side of the highway, where you will see the view from Little Stony Point.

TROPHY POINT BATTLE MONUMENT, WEST POINT *(page 95)* and STORM KING & BREAKNECK RIDGE *(page 98–99)*

Follow Route 9 North to Peekskill. Just after the exit for the city, follow signs for the bridge and make a left, crossing a small bridge over the Annsville Creek, into a traffic circle. Follow signs in the traffic circle to the Bear Mountain Bridge. Cross over to the west side of the bridge, and follow Route 9W north, where there will be signs to the entrance of West Point. At the gate, ask for a map, or the most direct way to get to The Battle Monument.

BREAKNECK VIEWS, HUDSON HIGHLANDS *(pages 96–97)*

See above directions for Bannerman's Island. This photograph was taken from the north side of the tunnel on Route 9D just outside Cold Spring. In order to get this view, you first have to make a steep climb.

ICE FLOE SUNSET & STORM KING MOUNTAIN *(page 100)*

See directions to West Point, above. When you leave West Point by the Washington Gate, bear to the right and you will be on one of the most scenic drives in the region, Route 218 to the village of Cornwall. This road is closed during most of the

winter months as well as when there are heavy rains and there is a danger of landslides. The photograph was taken along this road.

LAKE KANAWAUKEE, HARRIMAN STATE PARK *(page 101)* and FIELD OF COLOR, HARRIMAN STATE PARK *(page 102)*

Take the Palisades Interstate Parkway north to exit 17. Park in the lot on the right, past the tollbooth. For further information about park hours, call 845·786·2701.

IONA MARSH IN WINTER NEAR BEAR MOUNTAIN BRIDGE *(page 103)*

See directions below to Bear Mountain Bridge.

From the Bear Mountain Park Visitors Center, located on Route 9W just south of the Bear Mountain Bridge, go approximately 2 miles further south and you will see a sign on the left side of the road for Iona Marsh. There is a sign marking the road to Iona Island.

APPROACHING STORM WITH VIEW OF IONA ISLAND *(page 104)*

This photograph was taken from Anthony's Nose. To get there, follow the white-blazed Appalachian Trail on Route 9D at the start of the border between Westchester and Putnam Counties, just off the Bear Mountain Bridge. The trail is very steep. Less than a half-mile along the way, the path widens. Bear to the right here and begin following the blue-blazed trail. Within about 15 minutes you will approach the summit of Anthony's Nose. (Note: If you are unable to park along Route 9D, there is a parking area at Bear Mountain State Park. This way, you will add a scenic walk across the bridge to your hike.)

### BEAR MOUNTAIN BRIDGE (page 105)

The bridge connects Orange and Rockland with Putnam and Westchester counties. Follow Route 9 North to Peekskill. Following signs to the bridge, make a left and cross the bridge over the Annsville Creek. Follow signs in the traffic circle to the Bear Mountain Bridge. The road (Route 9D) snakes up the mountain and offers spectacular views at every turn.

### HOOK MOUNTAIN (page 106)

Cross the Tappan Zee Bridge (see directions below for how to get there) and take exit 10 off the New York State Thruway. Follow signs to the village of Nyack. Nyack State Park begins at the end of Broadway in the village. There are signs for the Long Path which leads up the mountain, for those who want to hike there.

### TAPPAN ZEE BRIDGE (page 107)

There are several ways to reach this bridge, which connects Westchester and Rockland counties. The easiest way is to head north out of New York City, and pick up Route 87 (New York State Thruway). Follow the signs to the bridge.

### CROTON DAM (page 108)

Drive north on Route 9 and exit at Route 129, after Ossining (Westchester County). Turn right off the ramp, then left, onto Riverside Avenue at the next junction. Continue for half a mile and bear right, staying on Route 129. After another 2.3 miles past the Croton Diner, there is an entrance on the right to Croton Gorge Park. The first right turn after this park entrance is Croton Dam Road. After crossing the dam, park and enjoy the view.

MOSSY HEMLOCK ROOTS IN THE MONTE GLORIA AREA OF THE MIANUS RIVER GORGE PRESERVE (page 109), and BOULDERS IN THE MIANUS RIVER (pages 110–111)

Take Interstate 684 to exit 4 (Bedford, Westchester County). Drive east on Route 172, and after a mile or so, make a left onto Route 22 North. In the town of Bedford, bear to the right around the village green, staying on Route 172 (Pound Ridge

Road). After 1 mile, make a right at the traffic light onto Long Ridge Road (CT 104). After ½ mile, make another right onto Millers Road. Cross the bridge and turn left onto Mianus River Road. The entrance to the preserve is on the left, approximately ½ mile down the road.

### PHILIPSBURG MANOR (page 112)

Take Route 9 North to the village of Tarrytown. This State Historic Site is on the left side of the road, just south of town. There are signs to direct you.

### THE PALISADES AT STATE LINE LOOKOUT (page 113)

As you drive north from New York City on the Henry Hudson Parkway, you are under these fortress-like rocks. On the Palisades Interstate Parkway and Route 9W, you travel along the top of them. Wonderful panoramic views are to be enjoyed at various points along the journey into or out of New York City.

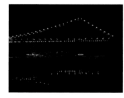

### NIGHT VIEW OF THE GEORGE WASHINGTON BRIDGE WITH MANHATTAN SKYLINE (page 114)

Take any bus from the Port Authority Bus Terminal in Manhattan that goes across the George Washington Bridge and stops at the Bridge Plaza bus stop. From there, go to the first cross street. Then walk south toward the river. You will see a visitors center, museum, and scenic overlooks as you approach the waterfront area. To the left of the museum, on Hudson Terrace, is the entrance to the Fort Lee Historic Park (open daily 9:30 AM–5 PM). Follow the steps that lead to the shore of the river, and to the remnants of the DuPont Dock, where this photograph was taken.

NEW YORK CITY SKYLINE *(page 116–117)* Take the New Jersey Turnpike to Exit 14B (Jersey City). Follow the signs to Liberty State Park from there. Ferry service runs from the Statue of Liberty and Ellis Island year-round. To find out the rates and schedules, call 212·262·5755 or 201·435·9499.